Crochet Flowers
for Every Wear

By Kooler Design Studio

Crochet Flowers for Every Wear

From head to toe, **pillows**, and throws, flowers appear "every wear" to add blooming fun to your world. Inside you'll find lots of **ideas** on how to add our **simple** crochet **patterned** flowers to everyday **accessories** for the home or fashion flair. Brighten up winter **scarves** or summery flip-flops with ease. With the sixteen simple flower patterns and a **bouquet** of yarns and beads you can accent anything and **everything** just like the projects shown. Or use this idea book to jumpstart your own **creative** designs as you spice up your life with colorful **crochet flowers**.

table of contents

Bouquet of Blossoms Pillow	4
Feminine Array Lamp Shade	5
Sea and Stars Lacy Scarf	6
Tropical Exuberance Pillows	7
Color Explosion Pillow & Scarf	8
Thick & Quick Purse	9
Bohemian Summer Kerchief	10
Hippie Hobo Bag	11
Cozy Rosy Accessories	12
Carpet of Roses Throw & Slippers	13
Funky Chunky Winter Fun	14
Happy Flowers from Head to Toe	15
Flower Burst Flip-Flops	16
Sweet & Cheery Sweater Set	17
Simply Smashing Fringed Sash	18
Velvet & Pinwheels Flowered Sash	19
Shower of Flowers Summer Dress	20
Spring Bouquet Headband	21
Pretty in Pink Bouquet T-shirt	22
Buttoned Up Cloche Hat	23
Flower Patterns for All Seasons	24
Crochet Basics	30
Useful Information	32
Materials Used in Models	34

bouquet of
blossoms pillow

A ready-made plump soft corduroy pillow gets a vintage look with the addition of bunches of pink flowers with jade-like green beads highlighting the centers.

finished size
6-Petal Flower (Large): 3"

materials

Worsted Weight Yarn
Small amounts per flower:
- Green
- Light Pink
- Peach
- Pink

- Crochet hook size H/8 (5 mm)
- Thirteen – 10 mm Green beads
- Needle
- Matching thread
- Beacon Fabri-Tac™ Permanent Adhesive

instructions

See page 25, 6-Petal Flower.

Make 13 flowers:

3 – Light Pink (A)/Peach (B)/Pink (C)
2 – Light Pink (A)/Pink (B)/Peach (C)
2 – Pink (A)/Peach (B)/Light Pink (C)
2 – Pink (A)/Light Pink (B)/Peach (C)
2 – Peach (A)/Pink (B)/Light Pink (C)
2 – Peach (A)/Light Pink (B)/Pink (C)

See page 27, Leaf.

Make 12 leaves:

12 – Green

Make 13 flowers, alternating the three Pink colors.

Sew or glue flowers and leaves onto pillow. Add a Green jade-like bead to center of flowers by sewing or gluing on.

feminine array
lamp shade

A vintage look is achieved by adding pale and delicate flowers to a ready-made fabric slip-covered lamp shade perched atop a milky glass lamp (both from a discount store).

finished sizes
9-Petal Flower: 1"
Buttercup: 2¼"
Daffodil: 1½"

materials
- Size 3, 100% Cotton Crochet Thread
  Small amounts per flower:
  Light Pink
  Light Green
  Pink
  Off White
  Tan
- Crochet hook size G/6 (3.75 mm)
- Beacon Fabri-Tac™ Permanent Adhesive

instructions
See page 26, 9-Petal Flower.
Make 3 flowers:
1 – Light Green (A)/Light Pink (B)
2 – Light Green (A)/Pink (B)

See page 24, Buttercup.
Make 8 flowers:
3 – Light Green (A)/Light Pink (B)
3 – Light Pink (A)/Off White (B)
2 – Pink (A)/Tan (B)

See page 28, Daffodil.
Make 9 flowers:
3 – Light Pink (A)/Off White (B)
3 – Pink (A)/Light Green (B)
3 – Pink (A)/Light Pink (B)

Using fabric glue, adhere flowers all around the top of shade, making a grouping at the front of shade as shown in the photo.

sea and stars
lacy scarf

Like little starfish clinging to the shore, these delicate and shiny star flowers sewn onto the edges of a lacy scarf turn it into a one-of-a-kind fashion statement with a look as fresh as a sea breeze.

finished size
Star Flower: 2"

materials
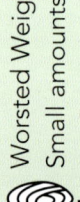
Worsted Weight Yarn
Small amounts per flower:
- Aqua
- Green
- Pink
- Teal
- Crochet hook size G/6 (4 mm)
- Needle
- Matching thread

instructions
See page 28, Star Flower.
Make **9 flowers**:
3 – Green (A)/Pink (B)
3 – Aqua (A)/Teal (B)
3 – Pink (A)/Aqua (B);

Sew flowers to the edges of scarf and one in the middle of scarf

tropical exuberance
pillows

Brighten up sun room or wicker patio furniture with these funky raffia feel pillows made from dime-store place mats. The burst of fireworks style flowers in tropical colors makes a big statement about your style.

finished sizes
9-Petal Flower: 1½"
12-Petal Mum: 2¾"
Daffodil: 1½"

materials

Worsted Weight Yarn
Small amounts per flower:

Aqua
Gold
Light Green
Orange
Pink
Yellow
• Crochet hook size H/8 (5 mm)
• 4 mm green/gold beads
• Beacon Fabri-Tac™ Permanent Adhesive

instructions
See page 26, 9-Petal Flower.
Make 6 flowers:
3 – Pink (A)/Blue (B)
3 – Green (A)/Pink (B)

See page 25, 12-Petal Mum.
See page 31, instructions for loading beads.
Make 6 flowers:
3 – Yellow (A)/Blue (B) with beads
3 – Yellow (A)/Green (B) with beads

See page 28, Daffodil.
See page 31, instructions for loading beads.
Make 6 flowers:
3 – Yellow (A)/Gold (B)/Yellow (C) with beads
3 – Yellow (A)/Orange (B)/Yellow (C) with beads

free form stems
With blue ribbon and size H hook, make chains desired length to create free form stems and leaf for flowers.

Use adhesive to attach stems to pillows.

color explosion
pillow & scarf

Explode with color by adding black and yellow accented flowers to a bright scarf and pillow. Pop art in primary colors never looked this cheerful.

finished sizes
5-Petal Flower: 1½"
5-Petal Large Flower: 1¾"

materials
Light Worsted Weight Yarn
Small amounts per flower:

- Black
- Blue
- Green
- Orange
- Pink
- Purple
- Yellow
- Crochet hook size F/5 (3.75 mm)
- Beacon Fabri-Tac™ Permanent Adhesive

See page 27, 5-Petal Large Flower.
Make 14 flowers:
14 – Black

Thread the tail ends of the yellow center through a colored flower and a black flower and secure ends. Trim and adhere to pillow and scarf with adhesive as show in photo.

instructions
See page 27, 5-Petal Flower.
See page 27, Small Centers.
Make 14 flowers & centers:
3 – Blue
3 – Green
2 – Orange
3 – Pink
3 – Purple

thick & quick purse

These bright flowers are just the thing to bring this purse to life. A thick felted purse needs chunky and bright embellishments to complement its scale.

finished size
Jonquil: 2½" and 4".

materials
Bulky Weight Yarn
Small amounts per flower:
- Blue
- Green
- Purple
- Red
- Crochet hook size J/10 (6 mm)
- Needle
- Matching thread

instructions
See page 25, Jonquil.
See page 27, Center.

Make 3 flowers:
1 – Blue
1 – Purple
1 – Red (Large)

Make 3 centers:
3 – Green (Large)

Add green centers to flowers and pull yarn ends through back. Sew flowers onto purse with needle and thread.

bohemian
summer kerchief

Pretend you're a flower child by adding heavily beaded flowers to this eyelet kerchief. It's a busy Bohemian look that will mix and match with all the latest accessories.

finished size
5-Petal Flower: 1½"

materials
- Size 3, 100% Cotton Crochet Thread Small amounts per flower:
  Aqua
  Blue
  Light Green
  Light Orange
  Light Pink
  Orange
  Pink
- Steel crochet hook size 0 (3.25 mm)
- 4 mm beads:
  Amber, Yellow, Clear, Blue & Pink.
- Needle & matching thread or
- Beacon Fabri-Tac™ Permanent Adhesive

instructions
See page 27, 5-Petal Flower & Leaf.

See page 27, instructions for loading beads.

Make 11 flowers:
2 – Orange (A)/Light Orange (B) with Yellow beads
2 – Light Orange (A)/Orange (B) with Amber beads
2 – Pink (A)/Light Pink (B) with Clear beads
2 – Aqua (A)/Blue (B) with Blue beads
2 – Blue (A)/Aqua (B) with Blue beads
1 – Light Pink (A)/Pink (B) with Pink beads

Make 11 leaves.

Add 25 beads per flower (five per petal). Load onto B thread before beginning stitch flower. Add one bead to each outer stitch.

hippie hobo bag

Go retro and change a plain suede purse into a bright hippie hobo style bag with flowers reminiscent of granny squares.

finished size
Buttercup: 2¾"

materials

 Worsted Weight Yarn
Small amounts per flower:
Black
Lavender
Purple
Tan

- Crochet hook size G/6 (4 mm)
- Beacon Fabri-Tac™ Permanent Adhesive

instructions

See page 24, Buttercup.
Make 8 flowers:
2 – Lavender (A)/Tan (B)
2 – Tan (A)/Lavender (B)
2 – Purple (A)/Black (B)
2 – Black (A)/Purple (B)

Stack two flowers together and adhere with permanent fabric adhesive as shown in photo.

cozy rosy accessories

Spice up plain accessories and make them your own with monochromatic roses. Hats, scarves, and mittens ensembles start out as blank canvases, and you make them unique!

finished size
Spiral Rose: 2½"

materials
Worsted Weight Yarn
Small amounts per flower:
Cream
Lt. Mauve
Lt. Peach
Mauve
Peach
Tan
- Crochet hook size H/8 (5 mm)
- Needle
- Matching thread

instructions
See 28, Spiral Rose.
Make **18 flowers**:
3 – Cream
3 – Lt. Mauve
3 – Lt. Peach
3 – Mauve
3 – Peach
3 – Tan

Sprinkle flowers on accessories

carpet of roses
throw & slippers

A field of brilliant roses across your lap will bring a smile to your face every time you curl up with this fun and chunky throw.

finished size
Rose: 4"

materials
Bulky Weight Yarn Small amounts per flower:
Blue
Green (base)
Magenta
Purple
Red
- Crochet hook size J/10 (6 mm)
- Tapestry needle

instructions
See page 24, Rose.
Make 80 flowers.
20 – Blue petals with green bases
20 – Magenta petals with green bases
20 – Red petals with green bases
20 – Purple petals with green bases
63 – Green circle bases to connect flowers

assembly
Lay out flowers in any random order. Place the small green circles in the spaces at each of the corners. Make the connecting circles by following the Rose pattern base to the 3rd Round step of 32 stitches. With green yarn and tapestry needle sew the flowers and green circles together. Add two rows of double crochet with green yarn all around the outer edge of the completed afghan.

SLIPPERS
Crocheted roses add a burst of color to a pair of warm slippers to match your throw.

finished size
Rose: 4"

materials
Bulky Weight Yarn Small amounts per flower:
Green
Magenta
- Crochet hook size J/10 (6 mm)
- Beacon Fabri-Tac™ Permanent Adhesive

instructions
See page 24, Rose.
Make 2 flowers:
Base – Green
Petals – Magenta
Adhere onto slippers with fabric adhesive.

13

funky chunky
winter fun

Oversized roses and two-toned wagon wheels team up to accent this cozy ensemble that is sure to warm up any winter's day.

finished size
Wagon Wheel: 1¾"
Ruffled Rose: 3"

materials

Worsted Weight Yarn Small amounts per flower:
Tan
Light Blue
Dark Blue
Lavender
- Crochet hook size H/8 (5 mm)
- Needle
- Matching thread

instructions
See page 26, Wagon Wheel Flower.
Make 9 flowers:
3 – Tan (A)/Light Blue (B)
3 – Tan (A)/Dark Blue (B)
3 – Tan (A)/Lavender (B)

See page 24, Ruffled Rose.
Make 1 each:
Tan
Light Blue
Dark Blue
Lavender

Sew flowers onto accessories of matching colors as shown in photos.

happy flowers
from head to toe

Here's an outfit with a rosy attitude. It's hard to have a bad day when wearing these happy flowers from head to toe. The addition of gold and crystal bead centers makes this ensemble extra sparkly.

finished sizes
Spiral Rose: 2"
Forget-Me-Not: 1½"

materials

Worsted Weight Yarn
Small amounts per flower:
  Light pink
  Pink
  Tan
- Crochet hook size G/6 (4 mm)
- Fifteen – 9 mm round Gold Antique donut beads
- Fifteen – 6 mm Pink crystal faceted beads
- Beacon Fabri-Tac™ Permanent Adhesive

instructions
See page 28, Spiral Rose.
Make 15 flowers:
5 – Light Pink
5 – Pink
5 – Tan

See page 26, Forget-Me-Not.
Make 15 flowers:
5 – Light Pink
5 – Pink
5 – Tan

Arrange the flowers on projects and use washable fabric adhesive to attach flowers to boots, cap, and skirt. Add a Gold round antiqued donut bead and a Pink crystal faceted bead to the center of each forget-me-not using adhesive. See photo below.

flower burst
flip-flops

Turn your ordinary flip-flops into a fashion statement by adding a huge, shiny burst of color to make your toes look perfectly pretty. The ruffled mum in three colors is impossible to miss at the beach or around the pool.

finished size
Ruffled Mum: 3½"

materials
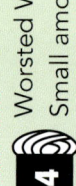
Worsted Weight Yarn
Small amounts per flower:
- Aqua
- Green
- Orange
- Red
- Yellow

- Crochet hook size E/4 (3.5 mm)
- Beacon Fabri-Tac™ Permanent Adhesive

instructions
See page 26, Ruffled Mum.
Make 6 flowers:
2 – Green (A)/Yellow (B)/Aqua (C)
2 – Pink (A)/Orange (B)/Red (C)
2 – Green (A)/Orange (B)/Pink (C)

Glue flowers to top of flip-flops.

sweet & cheery sweater set

Matching outfits never looked so good. Accent soft creamy sweaters for mom and baby with delightful sherbet-colored flowers for a look that's spring fresh.

finished sizes
5-Petal Flower: 1¼"
Buttercup: 2"

materials
- Size 3, 100% Cotton Crochet Thread
- Small amounts per flower & leaf:
  Blue
  Light Pink
  Off-White
  Orange
  Pink
  Sage Green
  White
  Yellow Green
- Crochet hook size E/4 (3.5 mm)
- Needle
- Matching thread

Sage Green (A)/Pink (B)
Blue (A)/Pink (B)
Yellow Green (A)/Orange (B)
Orange (A)/Light Pink (B)
Light Pink (A)/Pink (B)
White (A)/Blue (B)
Orange (A)/Blue (B)
Pink (A)/Yellow Green (B)

Make 12 leaves in Sage Green.

See page 24, Buttercup.
Make 12 flowers:
Yellow Green (A)/Pink (B)
Orange (A)/Yellow Green (B)
Pink (A)/Orange (B)
Light Pink (A)/Pink (B)
Blue (A)/Light Pink (B)
Pink (A)/Sage Green (B)
Pink (A)/Blue (B)
Blue (A)/Yellow Green (B)
Yellow Green (A)/White (B)
Pink (A)/White (B)
Sage Green (A)/Orange (B)
Orange (A) Blue (B)

Sew onto sweaters with matching thread as shown in photo.

instructions
See page 27, 5-Petal Flower & Leaf
Make 12 flowers:
Yellow Green (A)/Blue (B)
Yellow Green (A)/Pink (B)
Blue (A)/Yellow Green (B)
Pink (A)/Orange (B)

simply smashing
fringed sash

Go Bohemian with shiny contrasting flowers and turn a simple sash belt into a high fashion statement.

instructions

See page 26, 9-Petal Flower.

Make 6 flowers:
3 – Aqua (A)/Teal (B)
3 – Teal (A)/Green (B)

Sprinkle flowers on sash and sew on as shown in photo.

finished size
9-Petal Flower: 1¼"

materials

Worsted Weight Yarn
Small amounts per flower:
Aqua
Green
Teal
- Crochet hook size G/6 (4 mm)
- Needle
- Matching thread

velvet & pinwheels
flowered sash

Sprinkle delicate two-toned pinwheels onto a velvet belt or scarf to add a fun and funky 60s inspired touch to your ensemble.

instructions
See page 24, Pinwheel.

Make 5 flowers:
1 – Green (A)/Pink (B)/Green (A)
2 – Aqua (A)/Teal (B)/Aqua (A)
2 – Pink (A)/Aqua (B)/Pink (A)

Arrange on belt as shown in photo and sew on.

finished sizes
Pinwheel Flower: 1½"

materials

Worsted Weight Yarn
Small amounts per flower:

Aqua
Green
Pink
Teal

- Crochet hook size G/6 (4 mm)
- Needle
- Matching thread

shower of flowers
summer dress

A sprinkling of dainty flowers adds a special touch to this ruffled slip dress that any young miss will love. Using contrasting colors and adding tiny pearls to the centers of the flowers, you will be the picture of femininity.

finished sizes
5-Petal Flower: 1"
9-Petal Flower: 7/8"
Forget-Me-Not: 1 1/8"

materials
- 6-Strand 100% Cotton Embroidery Floss
  Small amounts per flower:
   Aqua
   Green
   Orange
   Pink
   Yellow
- Crochet hook size B/1 (2.25 mm)
- 5 mm pearls
- Needle & thread or adhesive.

instructions
See page 27, 5-Petal Flower.
Make 9 flowers:
Green (A)/Yellow (B)

See page 26, 9-Petal Flower.
Make 12 flowers:
2 – Orange (A)/Pink (B)
3 – Aqua (A)/Pink (B)
2 – Pink (A)/Aqua (B)
1 – Orange (A)/Aqua (B)
2 – Pink (A)/Orange (B)
2 – Aqua (A)/Orange (B)

See page 26, Forget-Me-Not.
Make 12 flowers:
4 – Orange
4 – Pink
4 – Green

Add a 5 mm pearl to the center of each flower and attach to dress with matching thread or adhesive.

spring bouquet
headband

Sweet and demure, this padded fabric headband is accented with a subtle and lacy sprinkling of flowers in pale colors.

finished sizes
9-Petal Flower: 1"
Buttercup: 2¼"
Pinwheel: 1¼"

materials
- Size 3, 100% Cotton Crochet Thread
  Small amounts per flower:
    Light Green
    Light Pink
    Off White
    Pink
    Tan
- Crochet hook size G/6 (3.75 mm)
- Beacon Fabri-Tac™ Permanent Adhesive

instructions
See page 26, 9-Petal Flower.
Make 4 flowers:
2 – Light Green (A)/Light Pink (B)
1 – Light Green (A)/Pink (B)*
1 – Light Pink (A)/Tan (B)

See page 24, Buttercup.
Make 1 flower:
1 – Pink (A)/Tan (B)*

See page 24, Pinwheel.
Make 2 flowers:
1 – Off White (A)/Tan (B)
1 – Tan (A)/Light Pink (B)

*Glue 9-Petal Flower to center of Buttercup.

Arrange and adhere to headband with fabric glue as shown in photo.

pretty in pink
bouquet t-shirt

Pretty and pink, this soft t-shirt top becomes unique and trendy when adding beaded flowers in many shades of pink.

See page 31, Instructions for loading beads.

Make 7 flowers:

1 – Light tan (A)/Tan (B) with Gold beads
1 – Tan (A)/Light Pink (B) with Red beads
1 – Pink (A)/ Medium Pink (B) with Red Beads
1 – Tan (A)/Pink (B) with White beads
1 – Light Pink (A)/Pink (B) with Gold beads
1 – Medium Pink (A)/Pink (B) with Red beads
1 – Medium Pink (A)/Light Pink (B) with White beads

Make 5 leaves.

Add a row of contrasting seed beads to outside edge of flower petals. Crochet a row of slip stitches with one bead on each stitch to outer edge of flower petals. Sew flowers and leaves onto t-shirt. See page 31.

finished size
Jonquil: 1¼"

materials
- 6-Strand 100% Cotton Embroidery Floss
  Small amounts per flower:
  Green
  Light Green
  Light Pink
  Light Tan
  Medium Pink
  Pink
  Tan
- Steel crochet hook size B/1 (2.25 mm)
- 3 mm seed beads in gold, Red and White
- Needle
- Matching thread

instructions
See page 25, Jonquil & Leaf page 27.

buttoned up
cloche hat

Give an early 1900s look to an angora hat by buttoning on simple thick worsted blooms that can be interchanged to suit your style and color ensemble.

finished size
6-Petal Buttonhole Flower: 2½"

materials

Worsted Weight Yarn
Small amounts per flower:

Blue
Green
Lavender
Light Blue
Light Green
Light Mauve
Mauve
Purple

- Crochet hook size G/6 (4 mm)
- Five – ⅝" buttons
- Needle
- Matching thread

instructions
See page 25, 6-Petal Buttonhole Flower.

Make 5 flowers:
1 – Light Blue (A)/Blue (B)
2 – Light Green (A)/Green (B)
1 – Light Mauve (A)/Mauve (B)
1 – Lavender (A)/Purple (B)

Sew bright-colored buttons onto hat and use to button on flowers. Make extra flowers in different colors to change the look of the hat by changing the flowers to match an outfit.

23

flower patterns
for all seasons

buttercup

With A, ch 6 and join with sl st in beg ch to form ring.
Rnd 1: 12 hdc into ring and join with sl st in beg hdc. Finish off.
Rnd 2: Attach B with sl st in any back loop. *Ch 4, sk 1, slip into next back loop; repeat from * around — 6 ch-4 spaces.
Rnd 3: (Sc, hdc, dc, tr, dc, hdc, sc) in each ch-4 sp — 6 petals.

ruffled rose

Ch 5 and join with sl st in beg ch to form ring.
Rnd 1: Ch 1, 6 sc into ring, 2 sc into beg ch 1. Place marker to show end of Rnd — 8 sc.
Note: Always work in back loop.
Rnd 2: 2 sc in each of the next 8 sc. Move marker — 16 sc.
Rnd 3: 2 sc in each of the next 16 sc. Move marker — 32 sc.
Rnd 4: *Sc in next sc, 2 sc in next sc; repeat from * around and remove marker. Finish off — 48 sc.

Petals

Rejoin with sl st into center loop (ch 2, 2 dc) in same loop, *3 dc into each loop around spiral. Finish off.

pinwheel 2-colored flower

With A, ch 6 and join with sl st in beg ch to form ring.
Rnd 1: Ch 1, 14 sc into ring, join with sl st in beg sc. Finish off — 14 sc.
Rnd 2: Attach B with sl st in next sc, sc in same sc, *ch 3, sk 1 sc, sc in next sc; repeat from * around ending with sl st in beg sc. Finish off — 7 ch-3 arches.
Rnd 3: Attach A with sl st into next skipped sc below arch, *sl st around ch-3 arch above, ch 4, remove hook from loop, insert hook into next skipped sc, pick up loop again, draw through and make sl st; repeat from * around ending with sl st in beg sc. Finish off.

rose

Base (Work in back loops.)
With A, ch 5 and join with sl st in beg ch to form ring.
Rnd 1: Ch 1, 6 sc into ring, 2 sc into beg ch 1. Place marker to mark end of Rnd — 8 sc.
Rnd 2: *2 sc in each sc around. Move marker — 16 sc.
Rnd 3: *2 sc in each sc around. Move marker — 32 sc.
Rnd 4: *2 sc in next sc, sc in next sc repeat from * around ending with sl st in next st. Finish off — 48 sc.

Petals

Attach B with sl st center loop, (ch 2, 4 dc in same loop), sk 1 loop, sl st in next loop, (sk 1 loop, 5 dc in next loop, sk 1 loop, sl 1 loop) 14 times. Finish off — 15 petals (no petals on outer edge).

24

12-petal mum

With A, ch 6 and join with sl st in beg ch to form ring.
Rnd 1: 12 sc into ring and join with sl st in beg sc. Finish off.
Rnd 2: Attach B with sl st in any sc, *ch 10, 2 sc in 2nd ch from hook. Sc in each of the next 8 sc and sl st back into same sc, sl st into next sc; repeat from * around. Finish off — 12 petals.

jonquil

Ch 6 and join with sl st in beg ch to form ring.
Rnd 1: 12 sc into ring and join with sl st in beg sc.
Rnd 2: *3 sc in next sc front loop, sl st into next front loop; repeat from * around — 6 petals.
Rnd 3: *Sl st into next loop behind petal, 3 sc in next loop behind sl st; repeat from * around ending with slip st in beg sl st. Finish off 6 petals.

Large Flower
Change outer petals from sc to dc.

Leaf
With A sl st into any back loop behind petals, ch 7, sl back into 2nd ch from hook, sc in next ch, hdc in next ch, dc in next 2 ch, dc, tr in last ch, sl st into beg sl st.

6-petal buttonhole flower

With A, ch 6 and join with sl st in beg ch to form ring.
Rnd 1: 18 sc into ring and join with sl st in beg sc. Finish off.
Rnd 2: Attach B with sl st into any back loop, *(2 hdc, 2 dc) in next sc, (2 dc, 2 hdc) in next sc, sl st in next ch; repeat from * around ending with sl st in beg sl st. Finish off — 6 petals.

6-petal flower

With A, ch 6 and join with sl st in beg ch to form ring.
Rnd 1: 18 sc into ring and join with sl st in beg sc. Finish off.
Rnd 2: Attach B with sl st into any back loop, *(2 hdc, 2 dc) in next sc, (2 dc, 2 hdc) in next sc, sl st in next ch; repeat from * around ending with sl st in beg sl st. Finish off — 6 petals.
Rnd 3: Attach C with sl st into back loop of next sl st, *5 dc in same st, sk next hdc, sc between next 2 dc; repeat from * around ending with sl st in beg sl st — 6 petals.

Leaf
With A sl st into any back loop behind petals, ch 7, sl back into 2nd ch from hook, sc in next ch, hdc in next ch, dc in next 2 ch, dc, tr in last ch, sl st into beg sl st.

wagon wheel flower

With A, ch 6 and join with sl st in beg ch to form ring.
Rnd 1: 16 sc into ring and join with sl st in beg sc. Finish off.
Rnd 2: Attach B with sl st in any sc, ch 2, dc in same sc, yo, insert hook in same sc, yo, insert hook in same sc pull through loop, yo insert hook in next sc pull through loop, yo, pull yarn through all 5 loops on hook. *Yo insert hook in same sc, pull through loop, yo insert hook in next sc pull through loop, yo pull yarn through all 5 loops on hook; repeat from * around ending with sl st in top of ch.

forget-me-not

Ch 5 and join with sl st in beg ch to form ring.
Rnd 1: (Ch 3, [yo, insert hook in ring pull up loop, yo pull through 2 loops] twice, yo pull through 3 loops on hook, chain 3, sl st around ring) 5 times. Finish off — 5 petals.

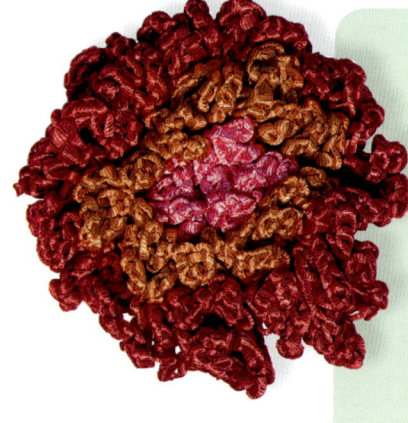

ruffled mum

With A, ch 6 and join with sl st in beg ch to form ring.
Rnd 1: 12 sc into ring and join with sl st in beg sc.
Rnd 2: * Ch 10, sl back into front loop, sl into front loop of next sc; repeat from * around. Finish off — 12 loops.
Rnd 3: Attach B with sl st into back loop of next sc, *2 sc in the same back loop of sc and 2 sc in each of the next 11 sc back loops; ending with sl into beg sc — 24 sc.
Rnd 4: *Ch 10, sl back into front loop of sc, sl into front loop of next sc; repeat from * around. Finish off — 24 loops. With C.
Rnds 5 & 6: Rep rounds 3 & 4 — 48 loops.

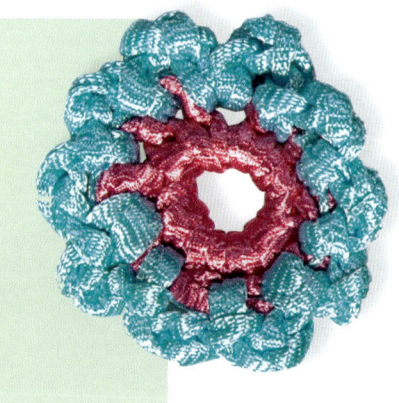

9-petal flower

With A, ch 5 and join with sl in beg ch to form ring.
Rnd 1: 9 sc into ring and join with sl st in beg sc. Finish off.
Rnd 2: Attach B with sl st in any sc, *ch 3, sl into next sc, repeat from * around. Finish off — 9 petals.

26

leaf

With A sl st into any back loop behind petals, ch 7, sl back into 2nd ch from hook, sc in next ch, hdc in next ch, dc in next 2 ch, dc, tr in last ch, sl st into beg sl st.

centers

Small Centers

Ch 5 and join with sl st in beg ch to form ring.
Rnd 1: 5 sc into ring and join with sl st in beg sc, pull tight. Finish off leaving 6" tail. Pull tail through flower center and secure on back.

Large Centers

Ch 5 and join with sl st in beg ch.
Rnd 1: 5 hdc in ring and join with sl st in beg hdc, pull tight. Finish off leaving 6" tail. Pull tail through flower center and secure on back.

5-petal flower

Small Flower

Ch 5 and join with sl st in beg ch to form ring.
Rnd 1: 5 sc into ring and join with sl st in beg sc.
Rnd 2: *(Sl 1, ch 2, 2 dc, ch 2, sl 1) in next sc; repeat from * around ending with sl st in beg st — 5 petals.

Large Flower

Ch 5 and join with sl st in beg ch to form ring.
Rnd 1: 5 hdc in ring and join with sl st in beg hdc.
Rnd 2: *(Sl 1, ch 3, 2 tr, ch 3, sl 1) in next hdc; repeat from * around ending with sl st in beg hdc. Finish off — 5 petals.

star flower

SPECIAL STITCH
Picot: ch 3 sl back in 3rd ch from hook.

With A, ch 6 and join with sl st in beg ch to form ring.
Rnd 1: Sc 10 into ring and join with sl st in beg sc. Finish off.
Rnd 2: Attach B with sl st in any sc, ch 4, sl back into same sc, *sl 2, ch 4, sl back into same sc; repeat from * around — 5 loops.
Rnd 3: *(Sc 3, picot, sc 3) around loop, sl 1, repeat from * around.
Finish off — 5 petals.

spiral rose

Ch 24 and join with sl st in beg ch to form ring.
Row 1: Sc in 2nd ch from hook, *(hdc, 2 dc, hdc) in next ch, sc in next ch; repeat from * across — 11 petals.
Using either end as center, wind strip around in a spiral to form rose, sew rounds to hold shape.

daffodil

With A, ch 5 and join with sl st in beg ch to form ring.
Rnd 1: 12 sc into ring and join with sl st in beg sc. Finish off.
Rnd 2: Attach B with sl st in any front loop, *sl 2, ch 3, sl back into 3rd ch from hook, repeat from * around ending with sl st in beg sl st. Finish off — 6 picots.
Rnd 3: Attach A with sl st into next back loop, *ch 3, sk 1, sl into next back loop; repeat from * around — 6 ch-3 spaces.
Rnd 4: Sl into first ch-3 space, *(hdc, 2 dc, hdc) in same sp, sl into next sp; repeat from * around. Finish off — 6 petals.

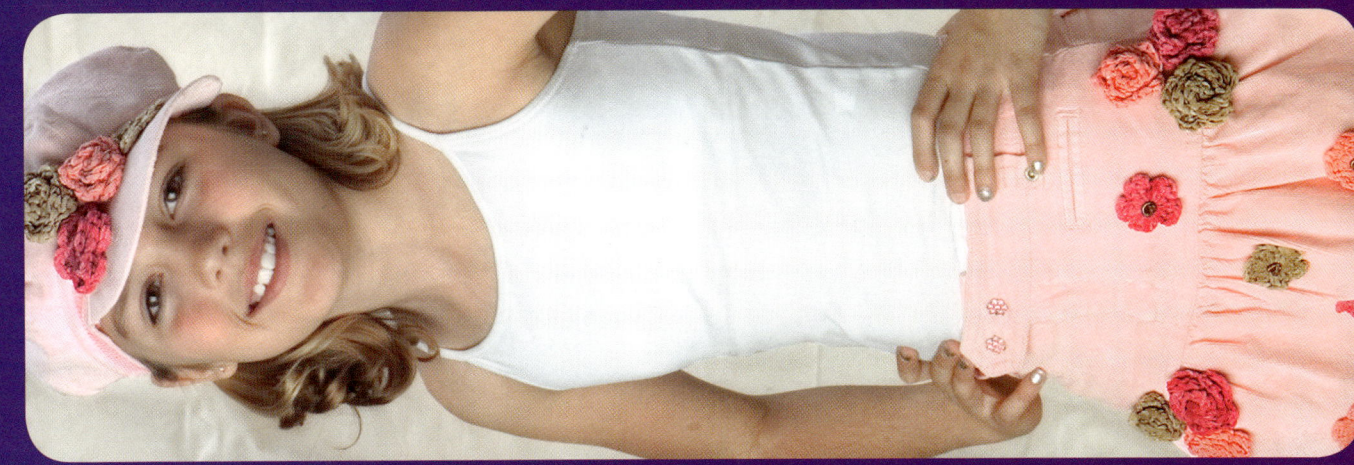

crochet basics

abbreviations

[ ] – work instructions within brackets as many times as directed

( ) – work instructions within parentheses as many times as directed

* – rep the instructions following the single asterisk as directed

" – inches
beg – begin(ning)
ch(s) – chain(s)
dc – double crochet
hdc – half double crochet
mm – millimeter(s)
rem – remain(ing)
rep – repeat
rnd(s) – round(s)
sc – single crochet
sk – skip
sl st – slip stitch
sp(s) – space(s)
st(s) – stitch(es)
tog – together
yo – yarn over (wrap yarn around hook)

making a chain

A chain starts with a slip knot (which does not count as a stitch). To make a chain, yarn over and pull through loop on hook.

1

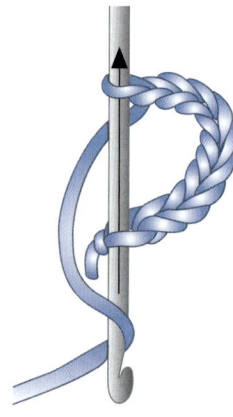
2

slip stitch

Insert hook, yarn over and pull loop through stitch and loop on hook.

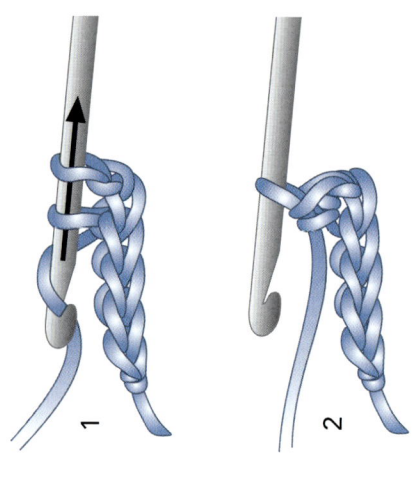

single crochet

Insert hook, yarn over and pull loop through, yarn over and pull through two loops on hook.

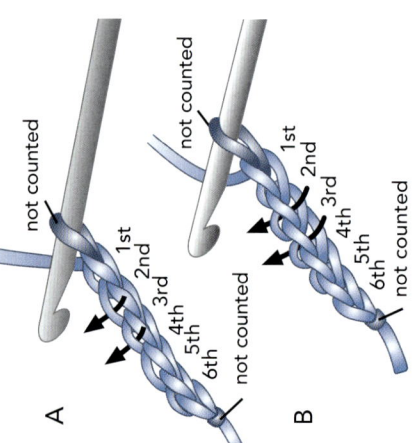
1

2

forming a chain ring

A chain ring is made by working a chain and joining it into a circle with a slip stitch. Then work into it or around it, catching up the tail as you go. If you are working into individual stitches, this is the ring you must use.

working in the chain

Method A: Insert hook under back loop of chain.
Method B: Insert hook under top two loops of chain.

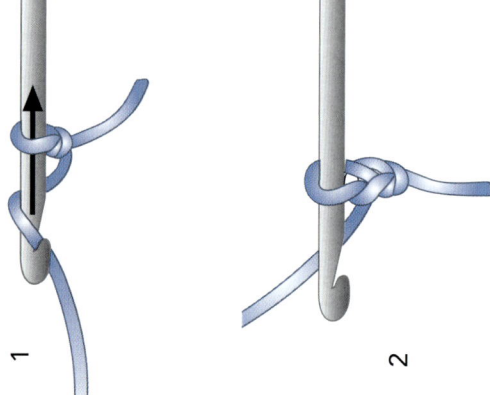

A   not counted 1st 2nd 3rd 4th 5th 6th
B   not counted 1st 2nd 3rd 4th 5th 6th not counted

front bead slip stitch

(fb-sl st): produces very densely packed beading. Insert the hook from back to front (wrong side to right side), push a bead up against the hook, yarn over, and draw through both loops.

loading beads on yarn

Cut a piece of wire 5" long and fold in half over the crochet yarn about 2" from the end. Trim ends of wire to even out and pinch "eye" end to secure the yarn (1). Thread beads on wire needle (2) and slide down onto yarn (3).

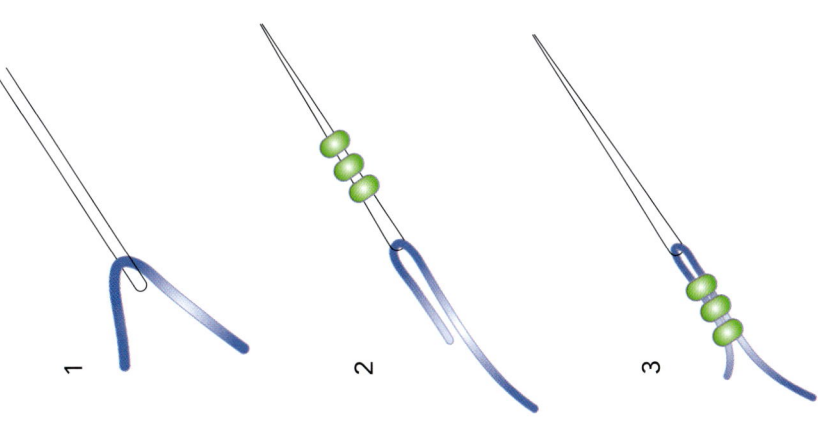

double crochet

Yarn over, insert hook, yarn over and pull loop through, yarn over and pull through two loops, yarn over and pull through rem two loops.

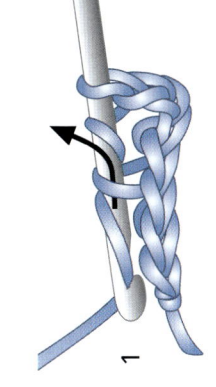
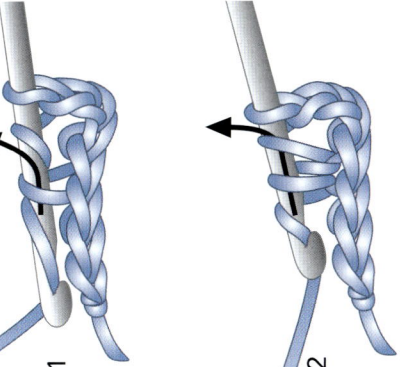

half double crochet

Yarn over and insert hook, yarn over and pull through loop. You will have three loops on hook. Yarn over and pull through all three loops on hook. You will have one loop remaining on hook ready to begin next stitch.

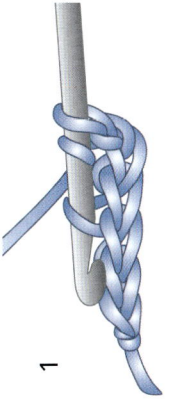
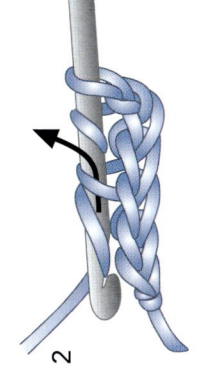

useful information

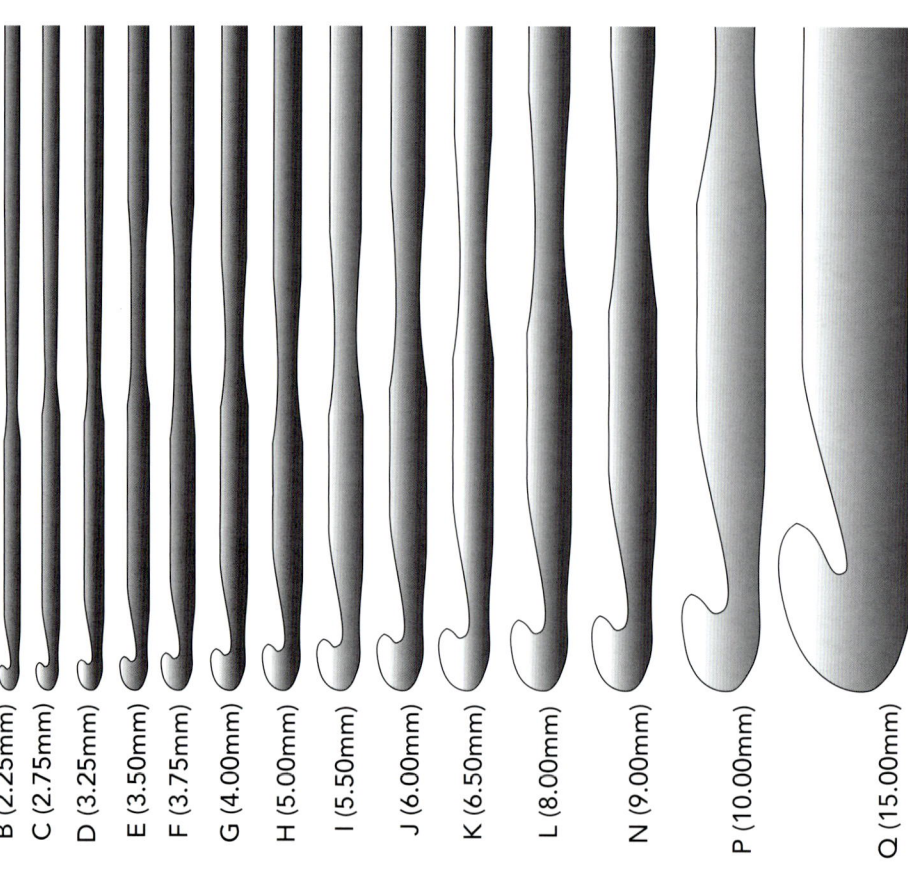

B (2.25mm)
C (2.75mm)
D (3.25mm)
E (3.50mm)
F (3.75mm)
G (4.00mm)
H (5.00mm)
I (5.50mm)
J (6.00mm)
K (6.50mm)
L (8.00mm)
N (9.00mm)
P (10.00mm)
Q (15.00mm)

crochet hook sizes

Millimeter Range	U.S. Size Range*
2.25 mm	B–1
2.75 mm	C–2
3.25 mm	D–3
3.5 mm	E–4
3.75 mm	F–5
4 mm	G–6
5 mm	H–8
5.5 mm	I–9
6 mm	J–10
6.5 mm	K–10½
8 mm	L–11
9 mm	N–13
10 mm	P–15
15 mm	Q

*Letter or number may vary. Rely on the millimeter (mm) size.

standard yarn weight system

Categories of yarn, gauge, and recommended needle and hook sizes

yarn weight symbol & category names	1 SUPER FINE	2 FINE	3 LIGHT	4 MEDIUM	5 BULKY	6 SUPER BULKY
type of yarns in catergory	sock, fingering, baby	sport, baby	DK, light worsted	worsted, afghan, aran	chunky, craft, rug	bulky, roving
crochet gauge* ranges in single crochet to 4 inch	21-32 sts	16-20 sts	12-17 sts	11-14 sts	8-11 sts	5-9 sts
recommended hook in metric size range	2.25-3.5 mm	3.5-4.5 mm	4.5-5.5 mm	5.5-6.5 mm	6.5-9 mm	9 mm and larger
recommended hook U.S. size range	B-1 to E-4	E-4 to G-7	G-7 to I-9	I-9 to K-10½	K-10½ to M-13	M-13 and larger

* Guidelines only: The above reflect the most commonly used gauges and needle or hook sizes for specific yarn categories.

materials used
in models

Bouquet of Blossoms Pillow p. 4
Worsted Weight Yarns
Pink
Lt. Pink
Peach
Mint Green

Feminine Array Lamp Shade p. 5
DMC – Senso 100% Cotton
#1101 Blanc
#1102 Old Gold
#1104 Light Baby Pink
#1105 Medium Rose
#1107 Nile Green

Sea and Stars Lacy Scarf p. 6
Anny Blatt – Victoria Ribbon
#282 Ketmie
#642 Menthol
#156 Celeste
#316 Lagon Bleu

Tropical Exuberance Pillows p. 7
Anny Blatt – Victoria Ribbon
#353 Miel
#482 Pastis
#092 Coloquinte
#282 Ketmie
#642 Menthol
#316 Lagon Bleu

Color Explosion Pillow & Scarf p. 8
Lion Brand – Microspun
#186 Mango
#158 Buttercup
#144 Lilac
#194 Lime
#103 Coral
#143 Lavender
#153 Ebony

Thick & Quick Purse p. 9
Lion Brand – Suede
#146 Fuchsia
#113 Scarlet
#132 Olive

Bohemian Summer Kerchief p. 10
DMC – Senso Microfiber Cotton
#1103 Medium Tangerine
#1104 Light Baby Pink
#1105 Medium Rose
#1106 Dark Autumn Gold
#1107 Nile Green
#1109 Light Peacock Blue
#1110 Medium Blue

Hippie Hobo Bag p. 11
Berroco –Suede
#3745 Calamity Jane
#3729 Zorro
#3714 Hopalong Cassidy
#3755 Wyatt Earp

Cozy Rosy Accessories p. 12
Worsted Weight Yarns
Tan
Cream
Mauve
Lt. Mauve
Peach
Lt. Peach

Carpet of Roses Throw & Slippers p. 13
Lion Brand – Suede
#110 Denim
#146 Fuchsia
#113 Scarlet
#140 Rose
#132 Olive

Funky Chunky Winter Fun p. 14
Berroco – Suede
#3704 Wrangler
#3787 Bat Masterson
#3714 Hopalong Cassidy
#3755 Wyatt Earp

Happy Flowers from Head to Toe p. 15
Berroco –Suede
#3754 Annie Oakley
#3753 Belle Star
#3714 Hopalong Cassidy

34

Pretty in Pink
Bouquet T-shirt p. 22

DMC – 6-Ply Embroidery Floss

Ecru
#165 Light Green
#470 Light Avocado Green
#776 Medium Pink
#951 Light Tawny
#957 Pale Geranium
#3771 Ultra Very Light Terra Cotta

Buttoned Up
Cloche Hat p. 23

Worsted Weight Yarn

Lt. Green
Green
Lt. Lavender
Lavender
Lt. Blue
Blue
Lt. Mauve
Mauve

Beacon Adhesives

Customer Service,
1-800-865-7238
Mt. Vernon, New York

Velvet & Pinwheels
Flowered Sash p. 19

Anny Blatt – Victoria Ribbon

#282 Ketmie
#642 Menthol
#156 Celeste
#316 Lagon Bleu

Shower of Flowers
Summer Dress p. 20

DMC – 6-Ply Embroidery Floss

#605 Very Light Cranberry
#964 Light Sea Green
#3825 Pale Pumpkin
#744 Pale Yellow
#471 Very Light Avocado Green

Spring Bouquet
Headband p. 21

DMC – Senso 100% Cotton

#1101 Blanc
#1102 Old Gold
#1104 Light Baby Pink
#1105 Medium Rose
#1107 Nile Green

Flower Burst
Flip-Flops p. 16

Anny Blatt – Victoria Ribbon

#482 Pastis
#092 Coloquinte
#507 Rouge
#282 Ketmie
#642 Menthol
#316 Lagon Bleu

Sweet & Cheery
Sweater Set p. 17

DMC – Senso Microfiber Cotton

#1101 Blanc
#1103 Medium Tangerine
#1104 Light Baby Pink
#1105 Medium Rose
#1107 Nile Green
#1109 Light Peacock Blue
DMC – Senso Wool/Cotton
#1303 Light Moss Green

Simply Smashing
Fringed Sash p. 18

Anny Blatt – Victoria Ribbon

#642 Menthol
#156 Celeste
#316 Lagon Bleu

notes

Produced by:

Kooler Design Studio
399 Taylor Blvd., Suite 104
Pleasant Hill, CA 94523
kds@koolerdesign.com

Production Team:
- Creative Director: Donna Kooler
- Editor-In-Chief: Judy Swager
- Technical Editor: Marsha Hinkson
- Writer, Book Designer, and Photo Stylist: Basha Kooler
- Production Artist: María A. Parrish
- Stitched Models: Helen Christensen
- Models: Chasidy, Thea, and Anna
- Photographer: Dianne Woods
- Proofreader: Char Randolph

Published by:

Copyright ©2006 by Leisure Arts, Inc.,
5701 Ranch Drive, Little Rock, AR 72223
www.leisurearts.com

We have made every effort to ensure that these instructions are accurate and complete. We cannot, however, be responsible for human error, typographical mistakes, or variation in individual work. This publication is protected under federal copyright laws. Reproduction or distribution of this publication or any other Leisure Arts publication, including publications which are out of print, is prohibited unless specifically authorized. This includes, but is not limited to, any form of reproduction or distribution on or through the internet, including posting, scanning, or e-mail transmission.

ISBN# 1-60140-086-1